CITIES AT WAR

BERLIN

★ ★ ★

Eleanor H. Ayer

new Discovery BOOKS

New York

Maxwell Macmillan Canada
Toronto

Maxwell Macmillan International
New York   Oxford   Singapore   Sydney

PHOTOGRAPHIC ACKNOWLEDGMENTS
Front Cover: Magnum Photos, Inc. (Ye Haldei)
Back Cover: The Bettmann Archive
Interiors: The Bettmann Archive: 4, 13, 14, 17, 18, 19, 21, 23, 24, 28,
    32, 33, 35, 36, 38, 40, 43, 44, 48, 50, 55, 56, 57, 61, 62, 67,
    71, 73, 74, 76, 78, 79, 81, 83, 84, 85, 88
    Magnum Photos, Inc.: (Erich Lessing) 26; (Ivan Shapin) 64, 68
    The Bettmann Archive/Hulton: 31, 47, 58, 72

New Discovery Books
Macmillan Publishing Company
866 Third Avenue
New York, NY 10022

Maxwell Macmillan Canada, Inc.
1200 Eglinton Avenue East
Suite 200
Don Mills, Ontario M3C 3N1

Macmillan Publishing Company is part of the Maxwell Communication
Group of Companies.

First Edition

Printed in the United States of America

10 9 8 7 6 5 4 3 2 1

Library of Congress Cataloging-in-Publication Data
Ayer, Eleanor H.
    Berlin / by Eleanor H. Ayer
        p.   cm. — (Cities at War).
    Includes bibliographical references.
    Summary: Examines the effects of World War II on the people of
Berlin, with emphasis on the city as the strategic center of Adolf Hitler's
Nazi government.
    ISBN 0-02-707800-0
    1. World War, 1939-1945—Germany—Berlin—Juvenile literature. 2.
World War, 1939-1945—Influence—Juvenile literature. 3. Berlin
(Germany)—History—Juvenile literature. [1. World War, 1939-1945—
Germany—Berlin. 2. Berlin (Germany)—History.] I. Title. II. Series.
D757.9.B4A94 1992
940.53'43155—dc20   91-29721

CONTENTS

★ ★ ★

The results of six years of war: Berliners walk through the streets of their demolished city.

★ ★ ★ ★ ★ ★ ★ ★ ★ ★

1

THE ARTIFICIAL CITY

It was Berlin's darkest hour. Six years of war had reduced Germany's showcase city to rubble. Its spacious streets, towering trees, and exquisite architecture now lay in blackened heaps throughout the capital. World War II had taken a toll on the city that even a year earlier would have been unthinkable to the German people.

Now on this Easter Sunday, April 1, 1945, the end of the German nation seemed likely. All that remained was for American, British, and Russian troops to close in on the capital city, to squeeze the last life out of Adolf Hitler's empire. That afternoon, England's prime minister, Winston Churchill, sat down to send a long message to American president Franklin D. Roosevelt. "I say quite frankly," his cable read, "that Berlin remains of high...importance. Nothing will [have the] psychological effect of despair upon all German forces...equal to that of the fall of Berlin. It will be the supreme signal of defeat to the German people."[1] Churchill knew the Germans well. Since their capital city's founding, Berlin had stood for all that was German.

For centuries, a large black bear with red claws has loomed in the center of Berlin's flag. Powerful and defiant, the bear stands tall on its huge hind legs. Since 1338, the Berlin Bear has been the symbol of its city's strength. But Berlin is even older than its bear. In 1987, the German capital celebrated its 750th birthday.

During the late 1100s, tribes of Germanic people roamed this region. As they wandered away to the west, groups of foreign fishermen moved onto the banks of the Spree River. Albert I the Bear, a native German, was unhappy with these foreigners invading his homeland, so he drove them out. The Bear became a hero. Years later, when it was time to choose a symbol for the growing city of

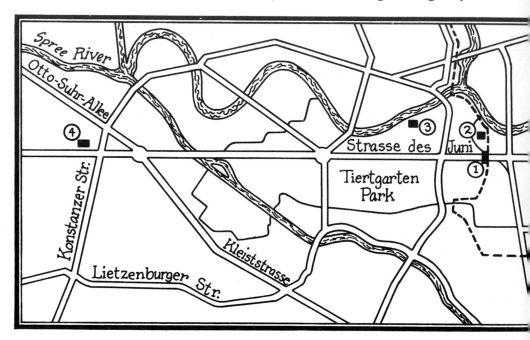

Berlin, Albert's followers remembered him. They chose a bear to stand for the city's strength.

Even in Albert's time, it was not unusual for Germans to be called warlike. As long ago as the first century, the Roman historian Tacitus had called them "proud, frank, and generous people." But he said German soldiers "became listless sluggards" without a war to fight, "for the Germans have no taste for peace."[2] In other words, Tacitus was saying that Germans are at their best in times of war.

Berlin became a northern outpost of the powerful Holy Roman Empire, which ruled over much of Europe from 962 to 1806. The government during this time was called the First Reich (pronounced *RIKE*), the German word for "empire." Rulers in different regions of the empire were called *margraves*, or governors. To help Berlin grow, the margraves built a travel route through the city.

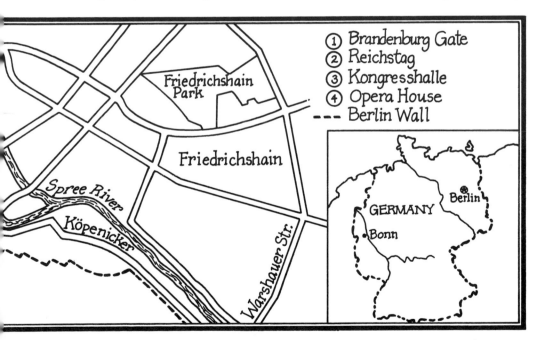

① Brandenburg Gate
② Reichstag
③ Kongresshalle
④ Opera House
--- Berlin Wall

They urged tradesmen to stop, set up stands to sell their wares, and stay for a few days. Berlin became a major trading center. Because leaders forced the city to grow quickly rather than letting it grow at its own rate, Berlin has since been called the "artificial city."

Shopkeepers and craftsmen across Germany formed guilds, which resembled today's labor unions. Each guild was made up of people in the same kind of business. To start a business, a person had to belong to a guild, and guild leaders ran most of the town's affairs. Not everyone could join, however. As early as the thirteenth century the Jews of Germany were treated unfairly. They were allowed to work only as money lenders or in jobs approved by the ruling class. In many parts of Germany, Jews formed their own guilds, but as soon as these guilds became strong, Christian bankers and tradesmen would have Jews banned from the town. Perhaps because Berlin was becoming a center of power, it treated its Jews more fairly than some other German towns.

In 1411, the region around Berlin came under the rule of the Hohenzollerns (*HO-un-zoll-erns*), a powerful family that soon made the city its capital. The Hohenzollerns, who would one day rule all of Germany, built palaces, public buildings, and parks; they invited artists and scholars to study in Berlin, and they increased trade with their neighbors.

While Berlin was expanding into a major city, people elsewhere in Europe were arguing fiercely over religion. About sixty miles south of Berlin, in the town of Wittenberg, a religious revolt was brewing that would one day affect the whole world. A local preacher, Martin Luther, and his followers were breaking away from the Catholic church to start the Protestant religion. They called themselves Lutherans and followed their leader's belief that people should live honestly and simply. But Luther was loud, rough, even violent about his ideas, and he loved Germany with the same passion that he hated Jews.

At first he spoke out against them for being hard to deal with, obstinate, and stubborn. Then in the mid-1500s, Luther published a pamphlet called *Von den Juden und ihren Lügen,* or *On the Jews and Their Lies.* In it he suggested that "synagogues should be set on fire....Jewish homes should be smashed and destroyed." The people, whom he called "poisonous, envenomed worms," should be "put...in a stable like gypsies, to teach them they are not master in our land."[3] This pamphlet was later called "a giant step forward on the road to the Holocaust"[4]—the murder of six million Jews during World War II.

Luther's wrath did not end there. He carried his anti-Semitism, or hatred of Jews, to other German cities. In Berlin, Lutherans raided and looted the city's synagogue. Luther finally convinced the government to ban Jews and expel them from the entire country. Many Jews who were forced to leave found new homes in Poland, Lithuania, and the Ukraine. Germans for many generations would share Martin Luther's brand of anti-Semitism—loving their country but hating its Jews.

By the late 1500s, many government leaders were realizing that they had made a mistake by exiling the Jews. In Eastern Europe, Jews were becoming successful in business and banking, making substantial contributions to their communities. Seeing what an asset the Jews could be to the business world, many German cities by the end of the century allowed Jews to return to their homeland.

Religious arguments throughout Europe turned to fighting in 1618 in what became known as the Thirty Years' War. The war began as a disagreement between Protestants and Catholics. During those thirty years, the Jews of Germany and Eastern Europe proved very helpful in raising money, finding food, and starting businesses to build the tools of war. Strangely, during the Thirty Years' War, Jews were treated better by their fellow Germans than at any earlier period. By the end of the war, Berlin was nearly destroyed, with more than a third of its houses in ruins. Smallpox, dysentery, and other illnesses killed nearly as many as the fighting, and the city lost more than half of its 12,000 people. At that time, the Thirty Years' War marked the lowest point in German history.

When the fighting finally ended, Berlin began a long period of rebuilding. People were so glad to be rid of the horrors of war that this became a time of greatness in writing, architecture, and music. Leading the German people through this period of growth and rebirth was a line of kings named Frederick. Frederick William, the Great Elector, came to power at the end of the Thirty Years' War and set out to expand the First Reich. Soon he had won an area called East Prussia away from nearby Poland.

Berlin was becoming an important center for government leaders, bankers, scholars, artists, and writers. Taking the throne in 1701 was the Great Elector's son, Frederick I, a frail, sickly, humpbacked fellow who spent his reign spending his people's money. Frederick I turned Berlin into a showplace, building elaborate palaces and schools, bringing formal French customs into his court, and running up a large debt. He paraded around his palace in red high-heeled shoes, hiding his deformed back with a waterfall of thick curls from his wig. "Crooked Fritz," Berliners called him, and he was hated or at least laughed at by most of his subjects.

Crooked Fritz's son, Frederick William I, put an end to his father's extravagant ways when he came to the throne. He focused his attention on building up the military and turning the Prussian army into the finest fighting force in Europe. Frederick William I gave Berliners a taste of what a military power the Hohenzollern empire would become.

In 1712, a child was born in Berlin to Frederick William I and his wife, Sophia. So special was this baby that his umbilical cord was put into a silver case with the words FREDERICK, PRINCE OF PRUSSIA AND ORANGE engraved on it. His parents called him Fritz, but to the rest of the world he would become known as Frederick the Great, one of the most famous of all German leaders. Fritz's father wanted the boy to study the science of warfare and to learn the military arts of fencing, riding, shooting, and precision drill.

"Wake-up time six o'clock," were the rules Fritz's father left with the boy's tutor. "He is to rise quickly and immediately...without turning over; then he shall kneel and say a little prayer....This done he shall put on his shoes and gaiters as fast as possible, wash hands and face, but not with soap....While he has his hair combed and tailed he shall take his tea at the same time as his breakfast."[5] So went Fritz's days until the boy finally revolted, for which his father beat him, pulled his hair, threw his beautiful clothing into the fire, and destroyed the precious flutes that the boy loved so much to play.

In spite of his father, this Berlin-born future king became the most popular ruler of his time. Frederick the Great brought a wonderful new age of music, philosophy, writing, and architecture to Berlin. One of his masterpieces was the finest opera house on the continent, which stood for 200 years until it was destroyed in World War II. Running east to west through their city Berliners built one of the most beautiful avenues of Europe, *Unter den Linden,* which means "Under the Linden Trees." In 1789, they began work on the Brandenburg Gate at the west end of the avenue. This gate, which took four years to build, became a symbol of Berlin's power and glory. The state of Prussia had become the most powerful of all the German states, and its capital was Berlin.

Berlin's rise was helped by the growth of railroads and industry. At a huge industrial fair in 1844, the city proudly displayed its strength—machines and manufacturing capabilities. Over the next twenty years, Berlin businessmen opened more than a thousand new factories. To make homes for all the workers, the city built cheap apartments, called tenements, that were extremely unsafe. Berlin became the largest tenement city in the world.

With the arrival of this new Age of Industry, the First Reich came to an end. On January 18, 1871, King Wilhelm I of Prussia became emperor of Germany. He took the title *Kaiser,* which is German for "Caesar," the great Roman leader and general. With the crowning of Kaiser Wilhelm I, a Hohenzollern became ruler of the entire German empire. This new period in Germany's history was called the Second Reich. It was the age of Otto von Bismarck, a political leader so concerned with building up Germany's industrial and military strength that he would be called the Iron Chancellor.

But Berliners and other Germans were about to pay a heavy price for their new military strength. During Bismarck's time, large landowners living in eastern Prussia were called Junkers. These were rude, narrow-minded people who thought they were better than other Germans. It was the Junkers who first talked of a "master race," a group made up only of "pure" Germans. No foreigners or Jews could be part of the master race. Otto von Bismarck was the most successful of all the Junkers. As the wealthy lord of many lands, he treated the people who worked for him like slaves. This was the way of the Junkers. They were cruel, selfish, and aggressive—seeking wealth and power at any cost. "The great questions of the day," Bismarck once said in a speech, "will not be settled by [rules] and votes...but by blood and iron."[6] The Nazis under Adolf Hitler would one day be much like the Junkers. They, too, would rule by "blood and iron."

While Bismarck was ruling as the first chancellor of the new German empire, William II came to the throne as emperor. Kaiser Wilhelm II, as he was called, had grown up loving the image of the powerful Prussian warrior-king, and as soon as he took over, he began pushing his military leaders to train for war. When trouble broke out between nearby Austria and Serbia in 1914, Wilhelm threw the might of his German armies behind Austria, a move that caused him to be blamed for starting World War I. Germany's defeat in 1918 spelled the end of the Hohenzollern rule and the end of the Second Reich—the second of the great German empires. At the end of World War I, Germany was a badly beaten nation.

Germans at a public soup kitchen after World War I.

For the next fifteen years, Germans paid a huge price for the warlike ways of their leaders. Poverty, hunger, and hopelessness overcame the people. Yet out of the ashes of the Second Reich would rise an even more warlike Germany. This new Third Reich, its capital still in Berlin, would bring the German nation to its darkest hour in history.

A young German boy gives flowers to Adolf Hitler, who many Germans believed would lead them out of the depression.

★ ★ ★ ★ ★ ★ ★ ★ ★

2

A SAVIOR FOR THE PEOPLE

The Germans were filled with hatred and bitterness as they tried to rebuild their country after World War I. People had lost pride in Germany and in themselves. Many were without jobs or money. During the winter of 1918-1919, nearly 300,000 people in Berlin alone were out of work. They were looking for someone to blame, but they were also looking for a leader and a hero.

To keep Germany from collapsing, government leaders met in the city of Weimar to write a new constitution. However, the Weimar Republic, as the government from 1919 to 1933 was called, turned out to be a weak government; it could not keep control. The Weimar years in Berlin, as in the rest of Germany, were wild and disorderly. In the city streets, political groups fought and rioted. In the beer halls, unemployed men sat sullenly talking and complaining, hoping for a strong leader who could help them out of their hopeless situation. Businesspeople who had once walked proudly and dressed smartly now tried to hide their worn-out clothes on the way to their offices. Outside Berlin, farms stood idle, their owners unable to meet their monthly payments.

German money was fast becoming worthless. Before the war, 4.2 German marks had been worth the same as one U.S. dollar. By 1923, it took 4.2 *trillion* marks to equal a dollar. On the streets of Berlin, housewives pushed wheelbarrows full of money to the store just to do one day's shopping. Men were sometimes paid twice a day so their wives could go grocery shopping at noon, before prices went up in the afternoon.

German teens were troubled to see their parents concerned only with finding jobs and making money. They seemed to have no other interests. Fifteen-year-old Horst Krüger lived in Eichkamp, a suburb of Berlin. He remembered the Weimar years as being "regulated, in order," in fact too much in order. "Get up at six thirty, wash, eat breakfast and put on a cheerful face, go to school, come home to dinner ... then my father's return [and] a feeble hope that something would happen—he might have brought something unusual from town. But nothing ever happened at our house....Sundays, of course, were always the worst....My parents' solemn, formal faces because it was Sunday."[1]

To help them restore pride in their country, young people turned to youth groups. For many years these groups had been strong in Germany. Members went hiking and camping together, sang and played guitars, wrote poetry, and read novels. Some groups were religious, some were military or political, and still others focused on nature. In each group, discipline was strict. By 1927, nearly five million young Germans belonged to youth groups. Many were unhappy with their country and their way of life.

Money to burn: a woman uses worthless German marks to fuel her stove.

Nazi soldiers make friends with the children of Berlin.

Jutta Rüdiger, who would later head the Nazi League of German Girls, said 1923 was the most important year of her childhood. That year there were political uprisings in the country. "One day some friends took me to a meeting of National Socialist students. I was greatly impressed....National Socialism meant comradeship—solidarity, you might call it today....And that's how I came to join the National Socialist German Students' League."[2]

Adults as well as teens wanted change. They wanted action, a cause to rally behind. Many of them began to see their answer in

Members of the Hitler Youth celebrate the birthday of their leader.

the leader of a rising political party called the National Socialist German Workers' Party (NSDAP), better known as Nazis. The leader, Adolf Hitler, was an Austrian who had fought proudly for Germany in World War I. No one had been more upset than he by Germany's defeat. The Weimar Republic, cried Hitler, was now dragging the great name of Germany in the mud. The kaiser's democratic government wasn't working. It was time to show force and strength. Hitler reminded Germans of the powerful military leaders from their past.

To rise to power, Hitler knew his party must win seats in the *Reichstag,* Germany's parliament. Nazi posters began appearing on buildings and streetlight poles. Heinz Kuehn was nearly nine when the Nazis started campaigning in Berlin. "During a stroll along Unter den Linden [we] spotted...an election poster showing the mustached face of the *Führer.* Father...lifted me up until I was face to face with Hitler's grim visage. 'Remember this face' he said. 'This man will some day destroy Germany.' "[3]

With banks failing and huge numbers of people out of work, families became desperate. The Nazis promised a better life, and people wanted to believe them. In the 1930 Reichstag elections, the NSDAP got more votes than ever before. The Nazis were on the rise. "Before 1933," recalled Wilhelm Fischer, "the Nazi salute was considered a joke. But we soon stopped laughing. I will never forget the first time I saw this salute....A streetcar came, and a fellow got out wearing a brown shirt, a red arm band with swastika, and leggings. He looked at a man standing next to me, they threw up their arms, and loudly shouted 'Heil Hitler!' I was 12 years old at the time and had no idea what it meant."[4] Soon all the world would know the Nazi straight-arm salute.

Hitler's next move was to put pressure on Germany's presi-

Hundreds of Berliners cheer at an early Nazi parade.

dent, Paul von Hindenburg, an old and sickly man. Hindenburg was worried and depressed because his Weimar government was failing the German people. Taking advantage of the president's weakness, Hitler began pushing Hindenburg to make him chancellor, the second most powerful position in the German government. Hindenburg said no. He was worried that if Hitler became chancellor, he would soon become an all-powerful dictator.

But millions of common Germans, especially young people, could see only promise in Adolf Hitler's becoming chancellor. "We loved the Fatherland and Hitler," wrote Inge Scholl, then a high-school student. "We heard on all sides [that he] would help the Fatherland achieve greatness, happiness, and prosperity and ensure that everyone had work and bread. He would not rest until every

German was free and happy."[5]

Seeing that there was nothing he could do to stop the Nazi tidal wave, Hindenburg at last gave in. On a wintry January 30, 1933, Adolf Hitler became chancellor of Germany. To celebrate, Joseph Goebbels (*GUR-bulz*), Nazi commander for Berlin, organized a torchlight parade through Brandenburg Gate. The Nazis used spectacular nighttime marches with flags, torches, and military music to get people to believe in their ideas and show off the party's strength.

Over Berlin Radio came voices proclaiming Germany's reawakening, promising that soon everything would be different and better. Across the Reich, flags with black swastikas began appearing in place of the black, white, and red flags of the former German empire. "It was a time of renewal," recalled 15-year-old Horst Krüger. "One day my mother came home with a small triangular pennant and said, 'That's for your bicycle. All the boys in Eichkamp have pretty pennants like this on their bicycles now.' " His mother had not been interested in politics, Horst explained. She was just so impressed by all the Nazi pomp that "she went to Hermann Tietz—he was...Jewish—and bought the first swastika pennant."[6]

In no time at all, Hindenburg's fears about Hitler began to come true. On February 4, just five days after he gained power, Hitler announced a new rule "for the protection of the German people." This rule allowed the Nazis to forbid meetings of other political groups. It also allowed the government to stop the publication of newspapers or magazines it felt were "harmful to the German people." What the new rule *really* meant was that the Nazis now had no competition. They could print what they pleased; there was no one to stop them.

*The Reichstag
on fire*

On February 24, Nazi police raided the Communist party headquarters in Berlin. During the raid they seized papers which they claimed were plans to overthrow the Nazi government. Three days later the Reichstag building, the government headquarters in Berlin, mysteriously caught fire. The Nazis blamed the Communists. They used the fire as an excuse to turn masses of German peo-

The new führer addresses his country.

ple against what they called "the Red Peril," and said the fire was a "God-given signal." Hitler told a London newspaper, "You are witnessing the beginning of a great new age in German history."[7] He was right about the new age; but it was to be one of horror, not greatness.

In a final move to destroy all competition, the Nazis declared the NSDAP the only legal political party in Germany. As Hindenburg had feared, Hitler had become a dictator. At a speech in Berlin, the Nazi leader announced that he planned to rebuild German military forces. Anyone listening carefully could have heard more in that message. Adolf Hitler was making it very clear that he did not intend to keep peace.

But millions of people were not listening carefully. All they heard was the promise of a great new Germany. Young people were particularly taken by the words of their Führer. They were born, he told them, to serve and die for the Fatherland. Kids around the country were ready; teens from Berlin to Bavaria began learning poems, songs, and verses of praise for their new savior, such as:

Your name, my Führer, is the happiness of youth;
your name, my Führer, is for us everlasting life....[8]

A few of the Volkswagens made before the factory began turning out arms for war.

★ ★ ★ ★ ★ ★ ★ ★ ★ ★

3

BERLINERS: JEWS, VOLK, AND NAZIS

itler had many ways of winning the hearts of the German people. At the Berlin Automobile Show of 1934, he introduced a new car that he guaranteed every German could afford. All a person had to do was buy five marks a week in government savings stamps. In just four years, a person would have saved enough to buy the new "peoples' car"—the Volkswagen. Millions of Germans saved, but only 210 VWs were built before the factory had to begin making tools of war.

By 1936, the Nazis were ready to show off their capital city to the world. All eyes were on Berlin during the summer Olympics that year. Max Mayer, who would later become a test pilot for the German air force, remembered the Berlin Olympics as "a whirlwind of

A sign on a German store reads: Jews Not Wanted

excitement. There was brilliant sunshine and a fantastic atmosphere....The crowds were [wildly excited]. Everyone was cheering."[1] It was exactly what the Nazis wanted. Jesse Owens, a black American athlete, won four gold medals in the Games. Hitler hoped the world would think Berlin was a city of fair and honest competition.

Nothing could have been further from the truth. The Nuremberg Laws, passed September 15, 1935, had made life as a German Jew a nightmare. Jews were no longer German citizens, nor could they marry "pure" (non-Jewish) Germans. It was illegal for a good German to do business with a Jew, to shop in Jewish stores, or to be seen by Jewish doctors and lawyers. The "Law against the Overcrowding of German Schools" meant that Jewish students could no longer attend public schools.

Many stores and even whole towns posted signs that said JEWS NOT ALLOWED or JEWS ENTER AT THEIR OWN RISK. But during the Olympics, these signs were taken down so visitors would think that Germany was a country of fairness and freedom under Hitler. The Nazis also stopped their persecution of the Jews—but only for the month of August while the Games were being held.

The truth was that Nazi Germany was fit only for Aryan or "racially pure" Germans. Aryan meant that your relatives for many generations had been good Germans—no Jewish blood and no foreign blood. It was best if you had blond hair, blue eyes, and light skin. Just in case there were any questions, the Nazis began teaching racial science classes in the schools. Students were supposed to learn how to identify Jews by the size of their noses and the shape of their heads.

Even the story of Cinderella took on a racial twist. Cinderella, the Nazis claimed, was a good German girl whose stepmother was wicked because she was a foreigner. The prince, a fine German lad, realized the the stepmother was racially impure and saved Cinderella from her horrible fate. A popular children's board game in Berlin and other German cities was "Get the Jews Out!" The instructions told players:

> *Be skillful when the dice you throw,*
> *and you'll collect Jews by the droves,*
> *If you succeed in throwing six Jews out,*
> *you're the winner without a doubt.*[2]

Not only were Jewish children banned from the schools, but Jewish teachers were fired and Jews were removed from all government jobs. In 1934, nearly one-fifth of Berlin's Jews were living in poverty, and by the end of the Olympic year more than half of the country's Jewish population was out of work.

For many, the only answer was to leave. Helen, a German-Jewish girl, was married the same year Hitler came to power. Under the Nuremberg Laws her husband, Siegfried, soon lost his job to the Nazis. Feeling they had no other choice, Helen and Siegfried made plans to leave for Holland. "The Nazis wanted to be rid of Jews, but they made it very difficult for us to leave. We had to fill out a great deal of paperwork....When moving day finally came, guards watched over everything that went into our large wooden boxes....We could take only a small amount of money out of the country....All this was hard, but the hardest part was saying goodbye to our parents, my 14-year-old brother and all our friends from childhood."[3] Many others did what Helen and Siegfried had done. From 1933 to 1939, nearly two-thirds of Germany's Jews left the country.

The police units ordered to search out and terrorize Jews were made up of some of the toughest, most ruthless Nazis. The SS

A group of Polish Jews expelled from Germany waits on the border of Poland.

Jews being forced to wash anti-Nazi slogans off walls

(*Schutzstaffel*) was the bodyguard for the NSDAP. These "Black-shirts" took their name from the color of their uniforms. Within the SS, the most feared of all units was the *Gestapo, Geheime Staatspolizei*, the State Secret Police. It was often the Gestapo that went from house to house searching out Jews in hiding.

Another police division of the Nazi party was the SA or *Sturmabteilung*—the storm troopers. Their nickname, the "Brown-shirts," also came from the color of their uniforms. Many who joined the SA had started their training in the Hitler Youth. This was the Third Reich's huge organization for young people. Hitler Youth members wore uniforms like the SA—brown shirts without the Nazi armband. There were three divisions of the *Hitlerjugend*: the *Jungvolk* for children 10-14, and two divisions for older teens, 14-16 and 16-18. In the early years of Nazi Germany, membership in the Hitler Youth was voluntary.

"Far from being forced to enter," remembered Alfons Heck,

A Jewish business is marked with a swastika

"I could barely wait. It seemed like such an exciting life, filled with 'duties' that were more like pleasures. Marching was something we could put up with for the fun of hiking, camping, war games in the field, and a constant emphasis on sports...." Even before membership in the Hitler Youth was required, more than six million boys and girls had joined. "Hitler always made us feel that we were his trusted helpers....We swore our oath to him with our left hand gripping the flag and three fingers of the right extended to the sky":

I promise in the Hitler Youth to do my duty
at all times in love and faithfulness
to help the Führer—so help me God.[4]

Reporter William Shirer recalled "many a weekend around Berlin [when] we would be interrupted in picnicking by Hitler Youths scrambling through the woods or over the heath, rifles at the ready and heavy army packs on their backs....Sometimes the young ladies would be playing at soldiering, too."[5] Much of the girls' training was like the boys'. But girls were taught that their most important duty to the Reich was to be healthy mothers of healthy Aryan German children.

Alfons Heck was one of 80,000 young people from across Germany seated in the stadium at Nuremberg on Saturday, September 10, the Day of the Hitler Youth. From his seat near the front he could watch Hitler's fist punch the air with short jabs while he spoke. It seemed to Alfons, as to every other boy and girl, that the führer was looking directly at him. Roaring into the microphone, Hitler told the crowd, "You, my youth, are our nation's most precious guarantee for a great future."[6] All 80,000 children in the stadium roared back in one voice to their führer, "Sieg Heil! Sieg Heil! Sieg Heil!"

The leaders of the Hitler Youth movement inspect a group of boys in Berlin.

Nazi soldiers with a carload of confiscated books to be burned.

"Each of us," said Alfons, "had a nearly hysterical feeling of national pride. For minutes on end we shouted at the top of our lungs, with tears streaming down our faces. From that moment on, I belonged to Adolf Hitler body and soul."[7]

Hitler had nearly the same effect on the *Volk*—the common people. At rallies in the Berlin Sports Palace and in speeches on national radio, Hitler told the Volk, "Finding you is what made my life's struggle possible." Not only had they changed his life, said Hitler, but he would change theirs as well. "You have found me. You have believed in me. This has given your life a new meaning, a new mission."[8]

Some Germans did not agree. One of them was the Protestant pastor Martin Niemöller, who was outraged by the way the Nazis were treating Jews. He was also afraid the government would outlaw Christianity. Niemöller organized the Pastors Emergency League. Soon several thousand people had joined. From his church in Berlin he promised, "No more will we keep silent; God commands us to speak. One must obey God rather than man."[9] Shortly thereafter, Niemöller was arrested by the Gestapo and thrown into a concentration camp, where he was held for seven years.

Throughout Berlin the tension was mounting. People were afraid to speak out, or even to make a joke about the government. The Gestapo seemed to be everywhere, watching the lives of all the Volk. Thousands of Nazi informers worked without pay, listening and watching for their neighbors to make a negative or questionable comment about the NSDAP. So many informers were there—one for every forty Germans—that people dared not trust even their own neighbors. You just never knew who might report you. Fathers were known to turn in their own sons for such "crimes" as listening to a foreign radio station. Often these "criminals" were sent to con-

German troops march into the Rhineland

centration camps from which they never returned.

Over the capital city, the storm clouds of war were getting darker. Hermann Göring, the Nazis' new air minister, planned to make Germany king of the skies in the air war he was sure would come. His office distributed fliers warning people to "Arm yourselves, form air-protection groups." Around Berlin posters appeared asking children to "Save your *pfennigs* for the RLB and live to grow up."[10] *RLB* stood for "Air Protection League" in German, a new group that organized civil defense programs.

The RLB taught people how to protect themselves in an air attack. Citizens learned to put screens over their windows to protect themselves from bomb fragments. Block wardens also showed people how to put up blackout cloth or paper in their windows so enemy aircraft could not spot targets at night. People could be sent to jail for not following blackout rules. To protect its citizens against poison gas, the government issued gas masks to people. Berlin schoolchildren practiced putting on the awkward masks and getting from their classrooms into air-raid shelters. Thanks to the RLB, by the time war did come, Berliners were ready.

Hitler took the first firm step on March 7, 1936, when his troops marched into the Rhineland along the German border with France. This part of Germany had been taken over by French troops after World War I. Hitler was determined to gain it back, and neither France nor any other country made a move to stop him. Even Hitler himself could not believe how easy it was. The Nazis won their first victory without losing a single soldier. The way was now open for war; Adolf Hitler could not be stopped.

★ ★ ★

Supporters wave Nazi flags as German soldiers enter Austria.

4

BERLINERS PREPARE FOR WAR

Their easy victory in the Rhineland gave the Nazis new faith. Austria would be next. Hitler had long wanted his Austrian homeland to be part of *Grossdeutschland,* "Greater Germany." At dawn on March 12, 1938, German troops moved across the Austrian border. His aim, said Hitler, was *Anschluss,* "reunification of the Germanic peoples." No one tried to stop him. In fact many Austrians were glad to see the troops. They welcomed Anschluss, for they admired the Nazis' power and wanted to become part of it. Austria was another easy victory for Adolf Hitler and brought nine million more people under his control.

Even Austria was not enough. Hitler next set his eye on a part of Czechoslovakia that poked into southeastern Germany. This area, the Sudetenland, was home to many people of German background. The Sudeten Germans wanted to be free from Czechoslovakia to govern themselves. Hitler supported them, but the Czech government's answer was a firm no. As if reading Hitler's mind, Czech leaders warned that they would fight back if Germany attacked. Hitler set October 1, 1938, as the deadline. Czechoslovakia must "set free" the Sudetenland or be attacked.

Not only did Hitler want the Sudetenland; he wanted war. But he could see that many Germans did not. To rally them, he ordered a parade through the streets of Berlin one late September evening, just as Berliners were heading home from work. The parade backfired, though, for fewer than 200 people gathered along the Wilhelmstrasse to watch. Reporter William Shirer was one of them. In his *Berlin Diary* he wrote, the people "ducked into subways, refused to look on, and the handful that did stood at the curb in utter silence....It has been the most striking demonstration against war I've ever seen." People simply did not want to face more fighting. Hitler "looked grim," Shirer said, and soon went back inside the Reich Chancellery. "What I've seen tonight almost rekindles a little faith in the German people. They are dead set against war."[1]

Nevertheless, on October 1, German troops marched into the Sudetenland. The Sudeten Germans, among them 17-year-old Peter Schober, welcomed the Nazis. "They were...greeted as Germans, and that was a big thing for us. We thought this was the right solution."[2]   And so, with the ease of his earlier victories, Adolf Hitler now had another 700,000 people under his control.

As his power increased, so did the danger for the Jews of Germany. Any doubt left in people's minds about Hitler's plan was dispelled on November 9, 1938. Two days earlier a young Jew,

*Flowers for the
führer: a young
girl greets Adolf
Hitler after the
occupation of the
Sudetenland.*

A synagogue burns during Kristallnacht

Herschel Grynszpan, had killed a German official in Paris. Grynszpan was upset because Germany was deporting all of its Polish Jews, his own family among them, and Herschel knew they would be killed.

The Nazis used Grynszpan's killing of the official as an excuse for a night of terror against all Jews in Germany. Across the country it was *Kristallnacht*, "the night of broken glass." Windows of Jewish shops were smashed and goods stolen or thrown into the street. Synagogues were set on fire and their contents destroyed. Jewish men and boys were rounded up, beaten, and hauled away in trucks to concentration camps.

Helen Waterford and her husband, Siegfried, who had fled to Holland to escape the Nazis, waited anxiously to hear what had happened to their families back in Germany on Kristallnacht. "Nearly every house was searched for Jewish men. The Nazi police, in plain clothes, came to my parents' apartment to arrest my father and 18-year-old brother. A 'helpful' neighbor had shown them where in the roomy attic some Jews could be hiding. My brother was deported to Buchenwald [a concentration camp near Weimar] as was Siegfried's brother, Hans."[3]

To be living in Germany as a Jew or even a half Jew, or *Mischling,* was frightening. Heinz Kuehn, a 19-year-old Mischling, was in Berlin on Kristallnacht. That evening as he walked home from a meeting he noticed a reddish glow in the sky and the smell of smoke. Approaching the Kurfurstendamm, central Berlin's shopping district, he heard "the crash of splintering glass and the sound of high-pitched voices harshly distorted by loudspeakers....Storm troopers on trucks, their yells magnified by bullhorns, were racing up and down the avenue. In one of the side streets a small synagogue was ablaze and the smell of smoke was intense. Here and there a cluster of policemen stood idle, watching indifferently...." Before Kristallnacht Heinz had hated the Nazis for their rude, rough, loud behavior. "Now...I feared them. From now on the sight of the Brownshirts [SA] and the Blackshirts [SS] made my heart pound and the palms of my hands sweat."[4]

Sensing that the worst was yet to come, Berliners used what time they had to prepare their city for war. Along the streets near

Brandenburg Gate they raised tall poles and stretched across them a brown and green camouflage netting which they hoped would make enemy bombers think they were flying over a forest. Works of art were packed carefully for storage underground, while statues and beautiful old buildings were fortified with sandbags. The city even held pretend "bombing raids"—complete with artificial smoke and bandaged "victims"—to give citizens a chance to practice for the real thing.

The real thing began at 6:30 A.M. on September 1. Eleven-year-old Alfons Heck was lying in bed. Soon his aunt would be in to wake him for a day of school and Hitler Youth activities. "I could hear the radio from the kitchen below. It was never turned on that early. There was a sudden fanfare blast of a *Sondermeldung*, a special bulletin, on the *Deutschlandsender,* the national radio network."[5]

When his aunt came into the room, he asked what was going on. Then he noticed the tears in her eyes. "Our troops went into Poland this morning," she replied quietly. "We are at war."[6] With that, Alfons jumped out of bed, wide awake and wildly excited, to get to Hitler Youth headquarters. Most adults, like Alfons's aunt, took the news quietly and sadly, fearful of where they were heading. It was *blitzkrieg*—"lightning war." As quickly as a flash of lightning, German armies took over Poland. In less than a month the country was under Nazi control. World War II had begun.

Ilse Koehn was a high school student in Berlin during the blitzkrieg. She was also a "Mischling, second degree," which meant that she had one Jewish grandparent. But Ilse did not know this. Her parents had never told her, feeling it would be safer for her not to know in case she was ever questioned by the Nazis. In school, everyone talked excitedly about the war. Germany's swift, sure victory over Poland had boosted students' faith in the Nazis. But at

home, Ilse did not hear this kind of excited talk. "My family said that Hitler was leading Germany to doom and destruction. Hitler said he was leading us to glory, and my classmates seemed to believe him. They eagerly listened to the radio broadcasts that in my home were shut off."[7]

Young Aryan Germans, like those in Ilse's class, seemed solidly behind Hitler. But many older Berliners were not so excited.

Citizens of Warsaw read the reports of Hitler's charges against their country.

German Jews, wearing yellow stars, try to flee their country before the fighting starts.

"War broke quietly, as if under a cloud," wrote reporter Warner Harz. "There were no frenzied people in the streets such as we read about in 1914. No flags, no processions. No cheering, no marching troops or flowers. The streets of Berlin seemed empty."[8]

After the conquest of Poland, Hitler told the Reichstag that Germany had "no further claims against France. Nowhere have I ever acted contrary to British interest."[9] Norway, Denmark, Sweden, and Finland were also safe, he said, but six months later, on April 9, 1940, German troops invaded Norway and Denmark. Hitler's promise to stay out of these countries had been a lie.

His promise to stay out of Belgium, Luxembourg, and Holland was also a lie. Helen and Siegfried were living in Amsterdam when the invasion of Holland began. "During the early morning of May 10, we were awakened by the roar and flak of hundreds of airplanes. The radio announced that German paratroopers had parachuted into Holland at 3 A.M. Some friends came over during the night. Together we did not feel so helpless. But we knew how desperate our situation was. There were serious discussions of suicide."[10]

It was blitzkrieg all over again. Not only did German troops attack the Low Countries, but they invaded France as well. Like the Dutch, the French fought back, but they were no match for Hitler's lightning forces. Germany seemed unstoppable. By May 24, French leaders admitted the war was lost. In one last, hopeless effort, French fighters bombed Berlin on June 7. But a week later their own capital city of Paris fell to the Germans. By June 25, two-thirds of France was under Nazi control. It looked now as if Hitler would soon rule all of Europe.

A Berlin house, the casualty of an Allied bombing raid.

5

A CITY UNDER SIEGE

Although much of Europe was easily overrun by Hitler, the Nazis found a tougher enemy in Britain. On August 25, 1940, the Royal Air Force (RAF) bombed Berlin. It was the first of dozens of British raids on the capital. During the next five years, Britain and its allies would drop more than 30,000 tons of bombs on the city, culminating in the Battle of Berlin.

Why Berlin? It was the capital city of the Third Reich, the home of hundreds of important government offices. Not only was this the largest city in Germany, it was the third largest in the world. Berlin was an important center of rail and boat shipping between Russia and Western Europe. One of the biggest reasons for bombing Berlin was its many huge factories that produced war materials.

Despite the nightly threat of bombing raids, Berliners were still able to lead fairly normal lives. Men went to work, children—that is *Aryan* children—went to school, and housewives tried to prepare nutritious meals in spite of food rationing. There was plenty of bread and potatoes, but fresh meat, fish, and fruit as well as sugar and even paper grocery sacks were hard to find. Coffee was more valuable than the German mark itself. German women talked of *Schlangestehen,* "standing in snakes," which meant waiting for hours in long lines to get food. People continued going to concerts, plays, and movies, although the choices were not always great. German historian Earl Beck recalled that "the worst selection was in Berlin, where sixty theaters were showing either *The Eternal Jew* or *Jew Süss,* propaganda films prepared for Goebbels's anti-Jewish action...."[1]

Berliners were so well prepared that none of the early raids did great damage. Antiaircraft gunners, often Hitler Youth members, were trained to shoot down enemy aircraft. Said one RAF pilot, "Berlin struck fear into the hearts of those crews ordered to attack it. It seemed to us that only the best German[s] were posted to defend it. [Every night a huge] cone of searchlights ringed the city....In all our...operations we [found] no target more heavily defended than Berlin."[2]

Most of the homes in the capital city were apartment buildings with attics on the top level. The government ordered people to remove whatever they had stored there. Attic walls were torn down so that fires could be reached easily and put out. Families were told to store fresh water and sand in their apartments. Berliners became experts at living in air-raid shelters, located in the basements of homes or business buildings. Every neighborhood had its shelter, and people assigned to that shelter came to know each other very well. They were proud of their temporary underground homes and fixed them up with furniture, kerosene lamps, bedding, books, radios, and all kinds of entertainment. As the bombings increased and raids began happening almost every night, women with small children or older people to care for would head for the shelters early in the evening to wait for the late-night raids. Folks caught away from their home shelters had to go into subway stations or other public places underground. A favorite spot for older teens was the basement of the Berlin Zoo, because its large supporting pillars provided a little privacy on a date.

Although air-raid shelters offered the best protection during bombing raids, they did not ensure safety. If the building was hit by a bomb, the shelter could collapse, killing everyone inside. Ilse Koehn, the Mischling, now a teenage *Hitlerjugend* member, worked hard helping victims during and after air raids. She was passing out sandwiches and coffee after one raid when the sirens began to wail again and the lights went out. "Take cover," voices screamed. "Into the cellar!" Through the darkness came the cries of small children, but the explosion of bombs drowned them out. "The walls began to shake; people screamed hysterically." Suddenly Ilse found herself frozen with fear, wondering if the ceiling of their shelter would cave in. "I began to think of my parents and of how worried they must be.... This is the end,' I thought. 'I'm going to die in this mass grave.' "[3]

It was not the end for Ilse. But Joseph Goebbels, the *Gauleiter* or "district leader" of Berlin, now ordered that all children must leave the city. Whole schools along with their teachers—nearly 800,000 women and children—headed east or into the mountains, away from RAF bombers. Ilse's school went to a small skiing village in the mountains of Nazi-held Czechoslovakia. "We've been told to pack for at least a year and to bring warm clothing," she wrote in her diary. *"Grossmutter* [grandmother] knits me a sweater after unravelling one of hers, and *Mutti* [mom] takes a day off to search for a pair of shoes for me. We have a special coupon entitling me to one pair of shoes. But every store we go to has either no shoes at all or not my size....One of *Grossvater's* [grandfather's] old jackets is made into one for me." As she prepared to leave, her grandfather walked Ilse down to the garden gate. "Little hedgehog," he said, "take care of yourself...."[4]

Upon arrival in their new home, Ilse and three other girls unpacked and stood staring out the window. "We are suddenly, utterly depressed," she wrote. "The mountains become barriers locking us in. We feel trapped, not knowing how long we will be here, alone and much too far from home. The uncertainty of the future, of everything, does not make it any better. A new girl joins us. I wonder how she feels. Her mother is dead."[5]

Not only did moving children out of the city protect them from war, it also meant that Berlin schools could be used as hospitals for the wounded and shelters for people who lost their homes in bombing raids. Fifteen-year-old Irma Krueger worked as a nurse in the building that had once been her school. "We auxiliaries—all girls in our teens—would arrive at our old school about seven in the morning....The wounded would already be there...stripped naked on the straw, covered with lice for the most part." Sprinklers in the ceiling would be turned on, Irma explained, to spray water on the men. "The doctors would be operating all day long, their rubber boots and aprons a bright red with blood, and our old school janitor, Herr Schmitz, would be back and forth all the time, carrying sawed-off limbs under his arms to be burned in the school incinerators in the cellar. It was a terrible time."[6]

Other groups of children were sent out of Berlin, but for a different reason. No one cared about their safety. It was hoped they would never return, and most did not. They were Jews, sent to Nazi

concentration camps to work or die. Across the Reich, the Nazis had built nearly 100 large concentration camps and hundreds of smaller ones. Thousands upon thousands of people died in these camps from disease, starvation, or torture. In all, 60,000 Berlin Jews were deported to concentration camps, where most of them died or were murdered.

Gestapo agents escort a group of Polish Jews to a concentration camp.

Fifteen-year-old Leo Fischelberg was deported to Bergen-Belsen, a concentration camp west of Berlin. His job was to unload the bodies of people who had died in the train cars on their way to the camp. "We carried them by their legs and arms and had to throw them onto a wagon, then bring them to an open pit and

German soldiers laugh at a Jewish family.

drop them in. I did this for five months....We once tried to take someone not completely dead and put him on top of the wagon so he could breathe. The Nazis beat us. We wanted to save a life, and they yelled at us, *'Schnell! Macht los!*—Quick! Get Going!' To them, to save a life was a waste of time."[7]

Large-scale killings were done at six extermination camps built by the Nazis in Poland. Unlike the concentration camps, these Polish death centers in the east were built especially to kill large numbers of people in a short time. Beginning in 1942, Jews were deported from Berlin to these extermination camps. They were

A train filled with Jews unloads at the dreaded gates of Auschwitz.

This photo, taken from the body of a dead German officer, shows a Nazi raid inside the Jewish ghetto in Warsaw.

rounded up by the Gestapo, often in the middle of the night, and herded to the nearest transit camp. In Berlin, the Levetzowstrasse synagogue was a transit center. Here 35,000 of the city's Jews were ordered to report for "resettlement to the east."[8] After reporting to the center, they would be loaded into cattle cars to make up a train. The railroads charged the SS a one-way fare for each passenger; guards on the trains had to buy round-trip tickets, for they would be coming back. Children under ten went for half fare, and those under four were free.

Being 16 years old meant the difference between life or instant death in an extermination camp. The Nazis thought children under 16 were too young to work. Unless they looked older or could tell a convincing lie, many younger teens were killed at once. Those 16 and older were sent to work camps. But conditions in the camps were so bad that thousands of these older teens died, too.

Prisoners were made to do backbreaking work in 12-hour shifts, stopping only once a day for a piece of dry bread and a small bowl of watery soup. "To be fifteen, sixteen years old and to be hungry day and night is something people don't understand," remembered Joseph Mandelbaum. "Once a day I ate that piece of bread and soup. I ate it so fast, I was afraid someone would take it from me."[9]

A very few of Berlin's Jews were able to survive the war staying right in the city. When Hitler first came to power, 160,000 Jews lived in the capital. As the Nazis tightened their grip on the city, the number declined; by 1941, fewer than 40,000 remained. That year the government made a rule that all Jews had to wear yellow stars sewn prominently on their clothing. Many chose not to follow this new order, for it seemed like certain death to wear the star. Some decided they would try to survive by living underground, which meant living in hiding. Shortly these Jews became known as "U-boats," for they could stay "underground" or "submerged" like the German submarines.

Across Germany, about 20,000 Jews went into hiding, 5,000 of them choosing to stay in Berlin, at the very center of the Nazi kingdom. With the help of courageous Germans who opposed the Nazis, about two-thirds of the Jews hiding in Germany survived the war. Wolfgang Hopp, a 14-year-old, was with his family when they submerged in Berlin. Helpful Germans found them places to live and stole important ration cards that were so necessary to get food in wartime Germany.

At first, few people were willing to help the Hopps, for they faced death themselves if they were found to be keeping Jews. One man, recalled Hopp, said no because "our Jewish corpses might be found in his apartment after an air raid." Like thousands of other Jews in hiding, members of the Hopp family moved from one house to the next, often having to live apart from one another. Wolfgang's father lived in a narrow room in a cousin's apartment, sleeping on a sofa "so small that I had to curl up like a question mark. Instead of talking I had to whisper; and when I walked I had to tiptoe. The room was cold, and for exercise I walked its length, a distance of about 12 feet, 25 times." Soon, Wolfgang joined his father in this tiny space, and for 21 months they never went outside.[10]

Because living in hiding meant staying inside and keeping quiet for months or years at a time, this plan did not work well with small children. Many Jewish youngsters were sent away, some to Aryan homes where it was hoped they would pass for a member of the family. Resistance workers—Aryans who risked their lives to help Jews in hiding—found homes for these children. When a home became available, the Jewish child would be taken immediately, sometimes never having a chance to say good-bye to his or her parents. Many Jewish parents gave up their children to total strangers, knowing they might never see them again.

Early in the war, while there was still time to get out, arrangements were made for a number of Jewish children to go to England. When a letter came for Karl Hartland, telling him that a place had been found for him in Ramsgate, England, Karl faced saying good-bye to what was left of his family. His mother was already dead. Now he had to leave the home that was so familiar, so com-

Concentration camp prisoners keep warm over fires fueled from the pile of boots taken from dead inmates.

A girl at Bergen-Belsen concentration camp is helped by a friend.

fortable to him. Only years later did Karl realize how lucky he was to have been able to leave. "If I had not caught the train to England...I would have been on one going to the Nazi death camps with millions of other Jews. Several members of my family perished, including my father and grandfather, and I know now that for me it was a near thing."[11]

The threat to Berlin's Jews from the British air attacks was now as great as the Nazi threat. The August 1943 air raid on the capital city was the beginning of the longest, steadiest attack on one target during all of World War II. It was the beginning of the Battle of Berlin, which would last through March 1944.

As death and destruction rained down on their city, Berlin teenagers grew up fast. Arno, a 14-year-old Hitler Youth member, recalled the night a bomber crashed in the bushes beside his grandmother's house. "[Grandma] told me there were some dead airmen. I just had to see them. [She] tried to stop me. 'Poor boys,' she said, 'they look so terrible.' But I had to see them....I remember their deathly pale faces, chalk white. These were the first dead men of the war I had seen, but I must say that I had a deep satisfaction....They were our enemies."[12]

Nearly one-third of the capital was destroyed in the eight-month Battle of Berlin. During the 19 air raids, 10,305 of the city's three million residents died. Yet for all their efforts, the Allies had not destroyed Berliners' spirits. People still had the will and the energy to rebuild and fight for their city, even though the tide of war had by now turned against them.

The mighty Reichstag falls to Allied bombs.

★★★★★★★★★★

6

TWILIGHT OF THE GODS

The Battle of Berlin greatly weakened the Nazis' grip on Europe. In the capital city and elsewhere across the Reich, people were losing faith in Hitler and his promise of total victory. Their homes were destroyed, food and fuel were gone, and nearly every family had buried a loved one lost in the war. In just three months during the summer of 1944, Germany suffered more than one million dead, wounded, or missing soldiers. To replace these troops, Berlin and other cities organized the *Volkssturm*, or "People's Militia." All men 16 to 65 years of age and women 17 to 50 were ordered to report for military duty.

In this spirit of defeat, people had very little enthusiasm for joining the Volkssturm. Still, no one dared speak out, for as Hitler saw his grip on the German people weakening, he enforced even stricter punishments for anti-Nazi talk. Even 14- to 16-year-old children were put to death for remarks against the Reich. Only the

Hitler Youth seemed willing—actually anxious—to fight. Walter Knappe, a Luftwaffe officer, was sent to Berlin to lead a unit of Hitler Youth against the approaching Russian army. "Only too well could I understand [the boys'] crazy enthusiasm; they went to their doom in the belief that they were fighting for Germany."[1]

It was *Götterdammerung* (GUH-tuh-da-muh-rung)—"twilight of the gods"—the beginning of the end for Nazi Germany. In mid-November the RAF began 16 more bombing raids against the capital. But now Berliners were unable to fight back. They shot down only 9 of the 402 aircraft that bombed them. By early February the Russians were just 50 miles from the capital.

On March 20, Hitler appeared in public for the last time to award medals to children who had shown special bravery in combat. Some of those Hitler Youth, among them Karl Damm, were the last defenders of Berlin. Karl's battalion was digging trenches about noon one day when the sergeant shouted to the boys to flee the area. "We grabbed our rifles and followed the sergeant toward the communications trench that would give us cover. But we stopped after only a few meters. The trench was occupied by our dead comrades—it was filled almost to the halfway mark with their bodies. Those were the first dead people I had ever seen in my life! But naked terror followed the horror. We stumbled over the comrades who had been mowed down, comrades we had gone through the past six months with. We were afraid to walk on the corpses, but we were even more afraid of joining them."[2]

By April 25, the Russians had surrounded Berlin—all they needed to do now was capture the city. Although Berlin was surrounded, Hitler refused to leave. "I cannot forsake the city which is the capital of this state....I wish to share a fate that millions of others have accepted....I have therefore decided to remain in Berlin....[I

*Adolf Hitler and
Eva Braun*

will] choose death voluntarily at the moment when I believe the res-
idence of the führer and the chancellor can no longer be held."[3]

In one of his last orders, Hitler named Admiral Karl Dönitz,
chief of the navy, to take his place as leader of Germany. Then in his
underground bunker beneath the Reich Chancellery in Berlin, he
married his girlfriend, Eva Braun. It was a short marriage. The next

German soldiers flee advancing Russian troops during the last hours of the war in Berlin.

day, April 30, 1945, Hitler dressed in a new Nazi uniform. After saying farewell to his staff, he and Eva went to their rooms and sat beside each other on a sofa.

Moments later a gunshot rang through the bunker. Adolf Hitler had shot himself in the mouth. He was dead. The Third Reich, which Hitler had boasted would last a thousand years, had only one more week to live. Eva swallowed a cyanide capsule and was also dead within minutes. Aides carried their bodies to a garden outside the bunker, poured gasoline on them, and burned them. By now Russian troops were firing on the Reich Chancellery. In the confusion, the remains of Hitler's and Eva's bodies were never found.

As Allied troops closed in to fire their final shots on the German nation, they discovered that their toughest enemies were the Hitler Youth, the last defenders of the Fatherland. But by now even these loyal fighters were beginning to feel fear. During the war, Alfons Heck had been proud of his position. Now, at 17, as he was about to be captured, his pride turned to terror that Allied soldiers would discover he had been a Hitler Youth leader. "Our enemies knew that the Hitler Youth were far more fanatic fighters than many adult soldiers." Alfons's fears came true when Allied soldiers threw him in jail and announced that he was sentenced to die by a firing squad at dawn. "That night for the first time, I felt betrayed by the man who had become my God....I realized then that we, the young fanatics of the Hitler Youth, had also become Adolf Hitler's victims."[4]

By May 2, Berlin was completely in Russian hands. Germans knew that of all the Allied soldiers, the Russians were the ones to fear most. During the war, German armies had nearly destroyed Leningrad, Moscow, and other Russian cities. Millions of people had died in the fighting and Berliners knew the Russians would be looking for revenge.

Ilse Koehn, the Mischling, back in Berlin from the mountain hideout with her schoolmates, joined her family in trying to escape from the Russians. For three days they lay on their stomachs in the crawl space under their house. Overhead they could hear the Russian tanks rolling by endlessly. "Russian voices continue laughing, cursing, commanding," Ilse later wrote in her diary. "There must be some Russians in our back yard. They're so close we can hear them breathe."[5]

As night fell again, she heard the sound of an accordion coming from her house. Hour after hour the Russians played and sang. "They must be dancing," whispered her mother. Then suddenly she realized, "They're drunk! My God, they're drunk. What will they do?"[6] Suddenly the sounds of broken glass, wild laughter, and gunshots filled the night. Around the city the scene was the same. Women and girls were being raped, houses and stores looted. Russian soldiers were getting revenge on their hated enemies.

Across the Reich, German troops were now giving up by the thousands. On May 7, 1945, General Alfred Jodl signed surrender papers for the German high command. World War II was over in Europe. Berlin, along with hundreds of other cities, lay in ruins. Berliners crawled from their air-raid shelters for the last time onto a horizon of horror. The city was a wasteland of burned-out buildings. One-seventh of all the rubble in Germany belonged to Berlin. Before the war, the city had had 245,000 buildings; 50,000 of those were now destroyed beyond repair. Streets were strewn with dead bodies—some of the 80,000 Berliners who had died for Hitler's dream. The city's population at the start of the war had been 4.3 million; now, with hundred of thousands dead or displaced across

The interior of the bombed Church of Our Lady

Europe, the population was down to 2.8 million.

Streetcars, Berlin's busiest mode of public transportation, were not running. One-third of the city's subway system was under water. There was no electricity or gas, and drinking water had to be hauled in from the country. So severe was the food shortage that starvation became a real threat. Much of the farmland around Berlin

One of Bergen-Belsen's ovens, where bodies of the dead were burned.

had been wasted by the war, so crops were destroyed. Hungry city dwellers grabbed what valuables they had left and headed for the country, where they hoped to trade their treasures for food. As the nights got colder, Berliners discovered another shortage: fuel. Coal supplies had been used up by the military. Sadly, the people began cutting trees along Unter den Linden and the city's other beautiful avenues. They would use the wood to keep warm during the coming winter.

As bad as things seemed to Berliners, there were people whose suffering was worse. Across the Reich, millions of concentration camp prisoners were still close to death. American troops under General George Patton were the first to reach them. When Patton's men marched through the gates of the first camp, they couldn't believe their eyes. So horrible was the scene—dead bodies thrown in huge piles, people nearly dead from torture and starvation—that General Patton vomited. He ordered his men to go into town and

German citizens forced to witness the horrors committed at a concentration camp.

73

Prisoners at Dachau cheer as Allied liberators enter the camp.

bring back all the Germans they could find. He made the towns-people walk through the camp and look at the horror. "We didn't know! We didn't know!" screamed many. But Patton and other Americans did not believe that people could live so close to the camps and not know what was happening in them. The mayor of the town was so upset (or scared) by what he saw that he and his wife went home and hanged themselves.

Millions of Germans at first refused to believe reports about the Nazi death camps. The pictures and stories were made up by the Allies, they said, just to make the Germans look evil. In jail after his capture, Alfons Heck was forced to watch films from the concentration camps, and he was one who refused to believe. "We thought they were fakes so we started to snigger and make comments like 'What do they take us for, monsters?' Our guards got very angry at this and started ramming us with rifle butts."[7] Alfons never faced the firing squad, but he and thousands of other German teenagers faced a lifetime sentence of a different kind. For as long as they lived, they would carry with them the burden of Nazi Germany.

The divided city

★★★★★★★★★

7

A CITY DIVIDED

At Potsdam, a city 20 miles southwest of Berlin, World War II ended and the Cold War began. Here Allied leaders from Britain, the United States, and the Soviet Union held their final meeting of the war. They agreed to divide Germany into four zones, one to be occupied by each of the Allies plus France. Because the Soviets had captured Berlin, they were assigned to the zone that included the capital city. This would have a great effect on the world in the coming years, for Berlin would become a symbol of the Cold War between Communist and free-world countries.

Like the rest of Germany, the capital was also divided into four sectors. Because Berlin was surrounded on all sides by the Soviet occupation zone, it was like an island in a Communist sea. For many people it was an island of grief and despair. The lack of food was greater now than it had been during the war, for there were no more Nazi-occupied countries from which the German government could take food.

German men and women work to clear some of the rubble from their streets.

Heinrich Gruber, director of a relief organization in Berlin, told a group of ministers just how bad the situation was in his city. "Men take their own lives out of despair. Thousands of corpses float down the Oder and Elbe into the sea; no one pays attention to it anymore. Thousands of corpses hang from trees in the forests surrounding Berlin...tens of thousands are on the roads, dying of hunger and exhaustion. Thousands haven't known for weeks, for

months, if they'll ever find a home again."[1] Of the 160,000 Jews who had lived in Berlin in 1933, just 7,247 remained.

Even U.S. President Harry Truman was shocked when he arrived in the capital city for the Potsdam conference: "Our drive took us past the *Tiergarten*, the ruins of the Reichstag, the German Foreign Office, the Sports Palace, and dozens of other sites that had been world-famous before the war. Now they were nothing more than

Life goes on: the people of Berlin view the damage done to their city.

piles of stone and rubble. A more depressing sight than that of the ruined buildings was the long, never-ending procession of old men, women, and children wandering aimlessly along the autobahn...carrying, pushing or pulling what was left of their belongings."[2]

Some Berliners, particularly the women, put aside their despair and began the long process of cleaning up and rebuilding. These "rubble women" were responsible for much of the city's cleanup after the war. Any brick or board that could be used to rebuild, the rubble women would clean or straighten. Slowly Berliners began to move back into temporary shelters for working and living. No one thought about the past or the future—only the present. It was day-to-day survival.

At first the Allies had no trouble traveling through Soviet Germany to reach Berlin. But by 1948, relations had become so tense that the Russians cut off all road, rail, and water routes into the Allied or western part of the city. Berlin was blockaded—cut off from food, fuel, and supplies.

The Soviet Union now split from the Allied group. The Cold War was growing much colder, and at the center of it stood Berlin. By blockading the capital, the Soviets hoped to drive the Allies out of the city. They wanted all of Berlin to be under Soviet control. If the blockade made Berliners hungry enough and desperate enough, thought the Soviets, they would agree to a Communist government. The plan didn't work.

On June 26, Allied pilots began the largest airlift in world history. Planes flew tons of food, fuel, and other supplies into Berlin. Crowds of children would gather on nearby hills to watch for what they called the "raisin bombers." Every day these Allied planes brought more food, coal, and machinery for Berliners.

For children caught in Berlin, Operation "Little Vittles"

Children eagerly await a plane that is part of "Operation Little Vittles."

made the difference between misery and a happy day. Lieutenant Gail Halverson, an airlift pilot, had spent much time in Europe during and after the war. He was impressed by German children, for they never seemed to beg in the streets. Deciding these kids deserved a treat, Halverson told a group of them to wait at the end of the runway when he flew in the following day and he would drop them gum and chocolate. Sure enough, as Halverson's plane flew over Tempelhof Airport the next day to drop supply bundles, several little handkerchief parachutes filled with treats floated down from his plane. The children told their friends, Halverson told his friends, and soon many more pilots were dropping treats to many more Berlin children. That year at Christmas, Halverson received more than 4,000 cards and letters of thanks from his new friends, who called him *Der Schokoladeflieger*, "the Chocolate Airman."

On May 4, 1949, the Soviets at last agreed to lift the Berlin blockade, but the end of the blockade brought the raising of the "Iron Curtain." An imaginary curtain of iron now separated east from west, dividing the free world from the Communist world. The two halves of Berlin became showcase cities for East and West Germany. In the west an economic miracle, the *Wirtschaftswunder*, was taking place. West Germans were working day and night to rebuild their country and their lives. After seven years of war, they once again had food, homes, jobs, and money. The "miracle" was possible thanks to the Marshall Plan, an American program of food, money, and machinery to help Europe rebuild after the war.

In East Germany there was no such miracle. The Soviets had no program like the Marshall Plan. Life was not getting better in the east, and it was becoming clear to Soviet leaders that the German people did not want them. On the free side of the country, Germans led much better lives than they did on the Communist

Soviet tanks move through the streets of Berlin's Russian sector.

side. More and more East Germans began escaping to the west, three-quarters of them through the capital city, which made Berlin an embarrassment to the Communists. By 1961, 3.5 million people had escaped.

The Communists knew that if they were to keep control of East Germany, these escapes must be stopped. Early on the morning of August 13, 1961, East Berlin police and workmen began tearing up streets along the border with West Berlin. They dug trenches,

East German young people look across into West Berlin.

strung barbed wire, and set concrete posts into the ground. A few days later it became clear what they were doing: A growing wall of bricks was sealing off East Berlin from West Berlin. No longer could East Germans cross into West Berlin, and West Germans now had to get special permits to enter East Germany. Suddenly friends and family were separated by the wall, no longer able to visit one another freely, and people were furious.

The Wall goes up: East German soldiers string barbed wire to make a border between East and West.

Over the years the Berlin Wall was made longer and stronger. When it was done, 28 miles of concrete divided East Berlin from West Berlin. Wire fencing was added, along with patrols, watchtowers and guard dogs. Checkpoints were set up along the wall where guards looked at people's passes very carefully. Sometimes travelers were held up for hours at the checkpoints or not allowed to cross at all. Even Westerners with special passes could stay in East Germany only a short time.

Almut Stepp was a West German teenager when she and her classmates visited East Berlin. "Everything was grey. Houses and buildings were all the same color. Very drab. It made us sad to look into East Germany....We could visit the east for just a short time. After that we had to pay for every day we stayed. We couldn't stay long because it cost too much."[3]

Anyone caught trying to escape along the wall would be shot. Still, East Germans continued to try. Over the years, 72 people died at the Berlin Wall, most of them shot by border guards. But some 5,000 more did make it safely to the West. For 28 years the Berlin Wall stood as the symbol of a divided city, a divided country, and a divided world. Communist countries were on one side, free-world countries on the other. When people spoke of the Cold War they thought of the Berlin Wall.

At last in the late 1970s there was a hint of a thaw in the Cold War. Soviet leader Mikhail Gorbachev opened the 1980s with ideas of *perestroika* ("reorganization") and *glasnost* ("greater openness") between East and West. Berliners welcomed glasnost, for they were ready to make their divided city whole again. On October 7, 1989, the fortieth birthday of East Germany, Communist leaders planned a celebration in Berlin. To their embarrassment, many East Germans picked that day to demonstrate against the government.

They wanted Erich Honecker, the country's harsh Communist leader since 1971, out of office, and they got their way. It looked as if the Cold War was near an end at last.

What happened next surprised everyone. On November 9, 51 years to the day after the Nazi Kristallnacht, the Berlin Wall was opened. The eastern side of the city was no longer sealed off from the west. Both East and West Berliners were wild with joy. An all-night party followed. Perfect strangers cried and hugged one another. Some drank champagne and danced on the wall, while others grabbed hammers and started breaking it down. After 28 years, Berliners could once again travel freely within their own city.

So happy were people that they hardly dared to ask the next question: Will the two Germanys unite again? With the Berlin Wall down, nothing seemed impossible. For the next seven months the eyes of the world were on Berlin. Finally on October 3, 1990, it happened. After 41 years of being divided, Germany was united once again.

For most Germans, unification was a glorious event. "I never thought I'd see it in my lifetime," said one Berliner. But many other Europeans, Jews, Russians, Americans—those who had suffered under the Nazis—were not so sure. They still saw Germans as being warlike people. A divided Germany was safer, they felt, less powerful, less likely to make war, less of a threat to the world. Although more than 50 years have passed since World War II began, the world will not let Berliners and other Germans forget their country's Nazi past.

Sabine Reichel is one of millions of Germans who weren't even born until after World War II, yet feel that they carry a burden of guilt for what their ancestors did. "It still isn't fun to be German," says Sabine. "It's a bit like having a...disease for which a cure

The Wall comes down: a young girl points happily to a crack in the Berlin Wall shortly before it is opened forever.

hasn't been found. History is a mean slasher. It hurts and haunts, leaving invisible scars. But sooner or later they burst open. A Nazi war criminal is caught...a photo of vile men in riding pants shoving children into cattle cars is printed somewhere...and I feel personally accused. In these moments I hate Germany."[4]

When Sabine's father first came face-to-face with American troops at the end of the war, he begged them, "Leave our children out of this, they're innocent." Sabine does not know what the soldiers answered. "But I do know that his plea didn't work. Sorry, Dad, but guilt can be a feeling, not a fact, and referring to my age never relieved me from the burden of my father's generation."[5]

SOURCE NOTES

✶ ✶ ✶

1. John Toland, *The Last 100 Days* (New York: Random House, 1966), 331.
2. Time-Life Books Editors, *Library of Nations: Germany* (London: Time-Life Books, 1984), 71-72.
3. Paul Johnson, *A History of the Jews* (New York: Harper & Row, 1987), 242.
4. Ibid., 242-243.
5. S. Fischer-Fabian, *Prussia's Glory* (New York: Macmillan, 1981), 136-138.
6. William L. Shirer, *The Rise and Fall of the Third Reich* (New York: Simon & Schuster, 1960), 94.

CHAPTER ONE

1. Horst Krüger, *A Crack in the Wall* (New York: Fromm International, 1986), 20.
2. Johannes Steinhoff, Peter Pechel, and Dennis Showalter, *Voices from the Third Reich* (Washington, D.C.: Regnery Gateway, 1989), xxvii.
3. Heinz R. Kuehn, *Mixed Blessings* (Athens, Georgia: University of Georgia Press, 1988), 34.
4. Steinhoff, Pechel, and Showalter, 36.
5. Inge Scholl, *Students against Tyranny* (Middletown, Connecticut: Wesleyan University Press, 1952), 18.
6. Krüger, 16.
7. Robert Goralski, *World War II Almanac* (New York: Bonanza, 1984), 19.
8. Charles Whiting, *The Home Front: Germany* (Chicago: Time-Life Books, 1982), 33.

CHAPTER TWO

1. Steinhoff, Pechel, and Showalter, 71.
2. Claudia Koonz, *Mothers in the Fatherland* (New York: St. Martin's Press, 1987), 219 (follows photo section).
3. Helen Waterford, *Commitment to the Dead* (Frederick, Colorado: Renaissance House, 1987), 15.
4. Alfons Heck, *A Child of Hitler* (Frederick, Colorado: Renaissance House, 1985), 9.
5. Shirer, 254.
6. Heck, 22-23.
7. Ibid.
8. Whiting, 22.
9. Martin Niemöller, *The Gestapo Defied* (London: William Hodge, 1941), 54.
10. Whiting, 46.

CHAPTER THREE

CHAPTER FOUR

1. William L. Shirer, *Berlin Diary* (New York: Alfred Knopf, 1941), 142-143.
2. Steinhoff, Pechel, and Showalter, 105-106.
3. Waterford, 26.
4. Kuehn, 57-58.
5. Alfons Heck, *The Burden of Hitler's Legacy* (Frederick, Colorado: Renaissance House, 1988), 65.
6. Ibid.
7. Ilse Koehn, *Mischling, Second Degree* (New York: Greenwillow, 1977), 34.
8. Whiting, 58.
9. Goralski, 97.
10. Waterford, 33.

CHAPTER FIVE

1. Earl R. Beck, *Under the Bombs* (Lexington: University Press of Kentucky, 1986), 46.
2. Martin Middlebrook, *The Berlin Raids* (London: Viking, 1988), 25-26.
3. Koehn, 99-100.
4. Ibid., 102-106.
5. Ibid.
6. Whiting, 68-69.
7. David A. Adler, *We Remember the Holocaust* (New York: Henry Holt, 1989), 70.
8. Barbara Rogasky, *Smoke and Ashes* (New York: Holiday House, 1988), 71.
9. Adler, 77.
10. Whiting, 99, 102.
11. Charles Hannam, *A Boy in That Situation* (New York: Harper & Row, 1977) 4, 146-147.
12. Middlebrook, 338.

CHAPTER SIX

1. Steinhoff, Pechel, and Showalter, 485-486.
2. Ibid., 476-477.
3. Shirer, 1125.
4. Heck, 202.
5. Koehn, 234-235.
6. Ibid.
7. Heck, 205.

CHAPTER SEVEN

1. Bernt Engelmann, *In Hitler's Germany* (New York: Pantheon Books, 1986), 330.
2. Robert J. Donovan, *The Second Victory* (Lanham, Maryland: Madison Books, 1987), 11.
3. Eleanor H. Ayer, *World Partners: Germany* (Vero Beach, Florida: Rourke, 1990), 54.
4. Sabine Reichel, *What Did You Do in the War, Daddy?* (New York: Hill and Wang, 1989), 3-4.
5. Ibid.

FURTHER READING

* * *

Adler, David A. *We Remember the Holocaust*. New York: Henry Holt, 1989.

Ayer, Eleanor H. *World Partners: Germany*. Vero Beach, Florida: Rourke, 1990.

Beck, Earl R. *Under the Bombs*. Lexington: University Press of Kentucky, 1986.

Chaikin, Miriam. *A Nightmare in History*. New York: Clarion, 1987.

Donovan, Robert J. *The Second Victory*. Lanham, Maryland: Madison, 1987.

Engelmann, Bernt. *In Hitler's Germany*. New York: Pantheon, 1986.

Fest, Winfried. *750 Years Berlin 1987 Information*. Berlin: Press-und Informationsamt des Landes Berlin, 1987.

Fischer-Fabian, S. *Prussia's Glory*. New York: Macmillan, 1981.

Gilbert, Martin. *The Holocaust: Maps and Photographs*. New York: Hill and Wang, 1978.

Goralski, Robert. *World War II Almanac*. New York: Bonanza, 1984.

Hannam, Charles. *A Boy in That Situation*. New York: Harper & Row, 1977.

Heck, Alfons. *A Child of Hitler*. Frederick, Colorado: Renaissance House, 1985.

———. *The Burden of Hitler's Legacy*. Frederick, Colorado: Renaissance House, 1988.

Jackson, Robert. *The Berlin Airlift*. Wellingborough, Northamptonshire, England: Patrick Stephens, 1988.

Johnson, Paul. *A History of the Jews*. New York: Harper & Row, 1987.

Koehn, Ilse. *Mischling, Second Degree*. New York: Greenwillow, 1977.

Koonz, Claudia. *Mothers in the Fatherland*. New York: St. Martin's Press, 1987.

Krüger, Horst. *A Crack in the Wall*. New York: Fromm International, 1986.

Kuehn, Heinz R. *Mixed Blessings*. Athens, Georgia, University of Georgia Press, 1988.

Laqueur, Walter. *Young Germany*. New Brunswick, N.J.: Transaction, 1984.

Mann, Golo. *The History of Germany Since 1789*. New York: Frederick A. Praeger, 1958.

Meltzer, Milton. *Rescue: The Story of How Gentiles Saved Jews in the Holocaust*. New York: Harper & Row, 1988.

Middlebrook, Martin. *The Berlin Raids*. London: Viking, 1988.

Niemöller, Martin. *The Gestapo Defied*. London: William Hodge, 1941.

Reichel, Sabine. *What Did You Do in the War, Daddy?* New York: Hill and Wang, 1989.

Rogasky, Barbara. *Smoke and Ashes*. New York: Holiday House, 1988.

Rossel, Seymour. *The Holocaust*. New York: Franklin Watts, 1989.

Russell, Francis. *The Horizon Concise History of Germany*. New York: American Heritage, 1973.

Scholl, Inge. *Students against Tyranny*. Middletown, Connecticut: Wesleyan University Press, 1952.

Shirer, William L. *Berlin Diary*. New York: Alfred Knopf, 1941.

———. *The Rise and Fall of the Third Reich*. New York: Simon & Schuster, 1960.

Steinhoff, Johannes, Peter Pechel and Dennis Showalter. *Voices from the Third Reich*. Washington, D.C.: Regnery Gateway, 1989.

Strawson, John. *The Battle for Berlin*. New York: Charles Scribner's Sons, 1974.

Time-Life Books Editors. *Library of Nations: Germany*. London: Time-Life Books, 1984.

Toland, John. *The Last 100 Days*. New York: Random House, 1966.

Waterford, Helen. *Commitment to the Dead*. Frederick, Colorado: Renaissance House, 1987.

Whiting, Charles. *The Home Front: Germany*. Chicago: Time-Life Books, 1982.

INDEX

✷ ✷ ✷